The Full Indian Rope Trick

Colette Bryce was born in Derry in 1970
and currently lives in Scotland.

Also by Colette Bryce

The Heel of Bernadette

Colette Bryce

The Full Indian Rope Trick

"spare, concise lyrics"

PICADOR

First published 2005 by Picador
an imprint of Pan Macmillan Ltd
Pan Macmillan, 20 New Wharf Road, London N1 9RR
Basingstoke and Oxford
Associated companies throughout the world
www.panmacmillan.com

ISBN 0 330 43597 3

9 8 7 6 5 4 3 2 1

A CIP catalogue record for this book is available from
the British Library.

Printed and bound in Great Britain by
Mackays of Chatham plc, Chatham, Kent

For my parents

my soul is rent and torn like yours
but it is beautiful because of that
like fine lace

YEHUDA AMICHAI

Acknowledgements

Independent on Sunday, The North, Oxford Poetry, Poetry London, Poetry Review, Riverrun, Bloodaxe Anthology of Contemporary Irish Poetry (Bloodaxe), *Breaking the Skin* (Black Mountain Press), *Forward Book of Poetry 2003* (Forward), *Hand in Hand* (Faber), *Out of Fashion* (Faber).

I'm grateful to the staff and directors of Hawthornden Castle, the Tyrone Guthrie Centre at Annaghmakerrig, and the Banff Centre for the Arts in Canada; to the Arts Council of England and the Society of Authors for timely financial support; and to the University of Dundee and the Scottish Arts Council for the fellowship in creative writing 2002–2005.

Contents

The Full Indian Rope Trick

Stones

We kept ourselves from children who were rich,
who were shaped in the folds of newest clothes,
who were strapped in the backs of foreign cars
whose quick electric windows rose
effortlessly, that poured into the stream of traffic;

but stared, fascinated, at their orthodontic
iron smiles, their nerve-averted eyes.

They were quiet. They feared rain. They were taught
to recite in yellow rooms *Colette, Suzette,*
Jo-jo and Lou are coming here for tea . . .
or to sing at the prompt of a tuning fork
How merry your life must be . . . ,

they had no idea, but disappeared
to the south of France twice a year –
as we ran the streets, the lanes and squares,
a band of outlaws, ne'er-do-wells
– then left for schools we didn't know.

From walls we saw them come and go.
War-daubed faces, feathers in our hair, wild,

we never smiled.

The Beast

I thought, to hear my mother talk,
corruption lurked
round every corner;
up back lanes, in the Bull Park shelter,
and nowhere more
than the high-rise walks
and stairwells of the Rossville Flats,
a den, she said, of iniquity –
levelled, now, to rubble.

I followed my nose for trouble;
and found my shadow racing me
along the dizzy balcony
of the seventh floor
and, chasing me,
the hound of hell, a vision –
its overgrown electric blue fur spiked
to lacquered peaks,
after the latest fashion.

Satellite

For all we see of you these days,
you might be living in outer space!
shouted my mother,
after my father, table cleared
of dinner plates, had poured a sea
of silver and coppers, metalfalls
from the money-drawer of the pub
where he'd spent the night before
pulling pints for the late drinkers.

We, his band of little helpers,
counted them into cityscapes
of stacks and towers – hours of fun –
our hands would turn an alien green
as, through the wall, their arguing
went on, my father circling,
there's nothing left
in this doom town for us;
my mother stood her ground.

Part of the task was to separate
the rogue harps and leaping fish
from the Queen's heads; the odd button;
even an errant dime or quarter
that had found its way across the water
bearing, on the backward swell
of the great Atlantic wishing well,
via the till of the Telstar Bar,
news of Brooklyn, or Manhattan.

And They Call It Lovely Derry

And so, strangely enough, to Florida.
Twenty from our side of the River
Foyle and twenty more from the other,
lifted out of a 'war-torn community'
to mix three weeks in a normal society.
That was the general idea.

When we arrived we were paired
and placed with a host couple, good
church people, settled and stable.
She was the first Prod I had ever met;
a small girl, pale and introvert, who wept
for home, then sniffed, and smiled.

The husband sat at the head of the table
holding forth, hot and bothered.
He couldn't decide on the right word,
hmmed and hawed between Blacks and Coloured,
whatever, his point? They were bone idle,
wouldn't accept the jobs they were offered.

The woman dreamed of having a child.
I took to the role of living doll
and would tolerate each morning's session
under the tug of curling tongs.
I had never even heard of Racism.
We gave a concert on the last night,

forty of us, rigid with stage fright.
My whistle shrieked on a high note.
We harmonized on all the songs
but fell apart with the grand finale,
the well-rehearsed 'O I know a wee spot . . .'
as the group split between London and Lovely.

The Smoke

The soul of the house was the one back room
to which his life had since retreated.

The soul of the room was the TV screen
that cast its blue and yellow light

that seemed when viewed from out in the night
like something close to flame.

My father sat alone, pipe
propped at an angle to inhale:

when smoke expelled – a dragon smile,
its scent of turf or heather fires,

the room about him stretched for miles.
It was slow dismantled, tipped and spilled

and tapped to empty, thumbed bowl full,
attended to by small soul-tools:

a blade, a spike, wires for the stem,
a tamping weight, a dipping flame.

The Deposition

Look how the faithful struggle with the body,
fumble for a pulse, all fingers and thumbs:
the cue balls of the eyes roll upward
in the skull; the skin glistens and stinks.
They are straightening the clothing
out of some sense of decency. Two of them
shoulder it, awkward, to the stairs,
a cruciform; the head lolling, jaw
faltering open on its hinge.
The feet trail, leave behind a slipper.
Staggering under its startling weight
of inanimate meat and bone under gravity,
they make it to the doorway, bed, deposit me,
leave me alone. They are true believers.
I am their mother. They trust me to rise
and find my way back, lie down in the body,
wake to inhabit another of my lives.

The Door

Hallowe'en; moonless, clouded.
Childhood opens the door to you,
races you through to a hall of screams.

Thirty years. All in a dream
you open the door to the face of a child;
shrouded, bloodless, hollow-eyed.

1981

A makeshift notice in the square
says it with numbers, each day higher.
North of here, in a maze of cells,
a man cowers, says it with hunger,
skin, bone, wrought to a bare
statement. Waiting, there are others.

Days give on to days; we stall
in twos and threes in the town centre,
talk it over, say it with anger,
What's the news? It's no better.
Headlines on the evening paper
spell it out in huge letters.

Over graves and funeral cars
the vast bays of colour say it
with flowers, flowers everywhere;
heads are bowed, as mute as theirs,
that will find a voice in the darker hours,
say it with stones, say it with fire.

Device

Some express themselves like this:
circuit kit; 4 double-A batteries, 1 9-volt,
1 SPDT mini-relay, 1 M-80
rocket engine, a solar ignitor,
a pair of contacts, 1 connector; wired,
coiled and crafted together, care
taken over positives and negatives.

Dawn or before, the artist's hour,
it is placed, delicately as a gift,
under a car in a street that will flare
to a gallery in the memory,
cordoned off and spotlit for eternity.

Last Night's Fires

The street lamp by the gutted bus
soft-ticks, watches us from the stuck
joint of its neck. There's windscreen
shattered on the ground like jewels,
diamonds, amethysts, on the school
walk. Bull Park; a wire mesh
and gravel pitch, some busted swings
bound tight about the bars.
Morning's finding morning hard.
Cars start, cough breath, raise
the lights of their eyes. A milk van,
faintly ringing. Then the fuel truck
with its damp sacks of slack
burdened on the deck; its skinny
truant rider; his cigarette, an ember.

Owl

Watching, over ditch and field,
against a twisted, stricken tree,
tell us, tell us, what did you see?

What stretched your wild witness eyes,
what warped your song to this hoarse cry
of *cruz*, this unrelenting cry?

What shut your mind against the light?

What knowledge so eclipsed your life
as the sun turned her face away?

What binds you to the darkness
of that day?

I am net. Soul caught.
I am night-swift instrument.
I am act borne of one thought:
blood must be atoned by blood.

The Message

The fish shot like a loose thought
out if its element, out of its world.
Shot? No, not quite . . . flipped
or hurled itself from the light-filled water,
took to the air with a helter-skelter
whirl, careered crazily

like a terrible insect hitting the ceiling
and walls with all of its dumb compulsion,
butting the pictures, mute under glass,
the Sacred Heart, the Weeping Rose,
the Virgin with her adult infant,
all our panic stations of the cross.

I raced to catch it, kept it in sight,
reached as you would for a butterfly,
ducked as you might from a swooping bat
in the cave of the room to which it had brought
the mayhem of a wayward pinball
ricocheted from point to point.

It paused, hovered, blurred in the air
like a hummingbird in lit suspension,
saw perhaps its gilded twin
in the flames and hurtled into the grate
where its nothing weight was vacuumed straight
up to the dark of the chimney space.

Kneeling, groping about in the soot,
I found it, flailing, sugared in grit,
and took it, dropped it onto the hearth,
half in disgust at the feel of its flesh
to the touch, half in a vague recall
that the human hand can scorch the form

of such a cold-blood creature.
And there it lay, still as a stone.
I noticed then its foetal detail,
the copperplated craft of it,
a gold smoke-blackened amulet,
and lifted it by the tip of its tail

into the bowl where it floated pale
and motionless at first, then twitched,
then gulped to life and circled, swam
calm as you like in its globe of water,
mouthing a message I couldn't catch
but thought about for a long time after.

The Full Indian Rope Trick

There was no secret
murmured down through a long line
of elect; no dark fakir, no flutter
of notes from a pipe,
no proof, no footage of it –
but I did it,

Guildhall Square, noon,
in front of everyone.
There were walls, bells, passers-by;
then a rope, thrown, caught by the sky
and me, young, up and away,
goodbye.

Goodbye, goodbye.
Thin air. First try.
A crowd hushed, squinting eyes
at a full sun. There
on the stones
the slack weight of a rope

coiled in a crate, a braid
eighteen summers long,
and me –
I'm long gone,
my one-off trick
unique, unequalled since.

And what would I tell them
given the chance?
It was painful; it took years.
I'm my own witness,
guardian of the fact
that I'm still here.

Pillar Talk

That magician
who stationed himself on a pillar

over Manhattan
for thirty-five hours

knows nothing whatever
of loneliness,

or how it is
for people like us

who have no soft acre
of cardboard boxes

not even the eggshell
flashbulbs of the press

or the well-meant antics
of neighbours with a mattress

to temper the thought
of the hard, hard earth,

to break the fall.
Nothing at all.

Blind Man's Buff

(Goya)

See how they dance in an eight-hand reel,
a symmetry of men and women, looks
and glances so many spokes
in a wheel – oh, to be one of them

and not this figure
blundering with bandaged eyes,
pierced with gazes, wondering
why every attempt at touch

meets with nothing much, with air.
Even the tree recoils. The lake stares
skyward. Only the mountains are aware,
admit to the permanence of the gesture.

Early Version

Our boat was slow to reach Bethsaida; winds oppressed us,
fast and cold, our hands were blistered from the oars.
We'd done to death our songs and jokes, with miles
to go, when Jesus spoke:

he said he'd crouched upon the shore, alone, engaged
in silent prayer, when, looking down, he started –
saw his own image crouching there. And when he leant
and dipped his hand

he swore he felt the fingers touch, and as he rose
the image stood and, slowly, each put out a foot
and took a step, and where they met, the weight of one
annulled the other;

then how he'd moved across the lake, walked on the soles
of his liquid self, and he described how cool it felt
on his aching, dusty feet; the way he'd strode a steady
course to board the boat

where we now sat – mesmerized. He gestured out
towards the shore, along the lake, then to himself,
and asked us all to visualize, to open what he always
called our 'fettered minds'.

The Word

He arrived, confused, in groups at the harbours,
walking unsteadily over the gangways;
turned up at airports, lost in the corridors,
shunted and shoved from Control to Security;
fell, blinking and bent, a live cargo
spilled from the darks of our lorries,
dirty-looking, disarranged, full of lies, lies,
full of wild stories – threats and guns and foreign wars;
or He simply appeared, as out of the ground,
as man, woman, infant, child, darkening doorways,
tugging at sleeves with *Lady, Mister, please, please* . . .

There were incidents; He would ask for it –
His broken English, guttural; swaying
His way through rush-hour trains, touching people,
causing trouble; peddling guilt in the market place,
His thousand hands demanding change, flocking
in rags to the steps of the church, milking
the faithful, blocking the porch, He was chased –
but arrived in greater numbers, needs misspelt
on scraps of paper, hungry, pushy, shifty, gypsy,
not comprehending *No* for an answer. What could we do?
We turned to the Word; called to our journalists, they heard

and hammered a word through the palms of His hands: SCAM.
They battered a word through the bones of His feet: CHEAT.
Blood from a bogus crown trickled down,
ran into His eyes and His mouth and His throat,
OUT: He gagged, but wouldn't leave.
We rounded Him up with riot police,
drove Him in vanloads out of our streets,
away from our cities, into the tomb
and left Him there, a job well done.
We are safer now, for much has changed,
now the Word is the law is a huge, immovable stone,

should He rise again.

Fabio's Miracle

The child saw it first, tripped screaming
from the alcove, grazed her knees.
I fell to mine and prayed to God,
La Madonnina wept. I ran for the priest.

They have come to expect the blood of a beast,
plastic arteries into the eyes, hidden
crimson cavities in the porous plaster, hairline
fractures loosening to a severed head,

a chip to the glaze of a lower lid
with the tip of a blade or the point of a pin,
dye applied like a girl's cosmetics,
streaked in the blaze of a midday sun,

but tests have been done: it is real blood.
Added to this, it is male blood.
The blood of the virgin ought to be female, no?
The blood of the risen Christ or the humble Fabio?

say the city men. They come and call me
charlatan. They say I've led the poor astray.
This woman, she was cured today.
That sound you hear, is that real prayer?

It's simple. We had nothing here
and prayed for bread. Now look around.
Let *them* survive on mountain air
and I'll say *It's a miracle!*

There are guards at the gate of our little chapel,
two brass keys to the small glass case,
one for the lawyer, one for the priest,
and no more answers, no more tests.

And since? I've visited just once. The queue
of pilgrims snaked for miles. I knelt and raised
my eyes to meet her raw, clawed face,
her livid gaze. One of us smiled.

The Negatives

I know I was there. I'm sure of it.
Or could I have imagined a day so fully?
I didn't leave early, when Lottie and Sylvie
had enough and called a cab from the village,

though I might have. I had an uneasy feeling
even then. I trusted the camera to the men,
I remember that, and the heat, the lake,
undressing; slipping the silk from my skin,

the soft water, clinging like silk
to our limbs, its lit, concentric rings.
Where have I gone? I search the prints.
There's Tom, arranging his suit on the grass

just so; as always, fastidious.
I tried one of Robert's black cigarettes
and coughed, then laughed, *cheroooots*,
he drawled, the word itself, delicious.

They are all there. The swans, fierce
by the broken cottage; William, enthralled.
Samuel, holding that stone that looked
like a skull, poor Yorick. The brimming well

where our coins fell, cut through the water,
sank in the mud into old tender.
I grip my wrist. Yes, it is real
with its ghost pulse, its pale blue rivers.

The chemist shrugged. He's an honest man.
I go back to the negatives, surely somewhere . . .?
raise them up to the future, bright
in the trinity of the long bay windows,

think of the film, coiled safe
in its vacuum case for all these years,
my image fading like frost, my face
a pattern vanishing on glass.

You begin, of course, to doubt yourself.
And now, there is only my word for it.
And who ever listens to an old woman
with the world still spinning so fast?

The Happy Retirement Balloon

One of the smokers found it,
laughed. It had blown in
to the space beneath the fire escape
and, trapped, couldn't keep still.
It was taut with a happy thought, one
of many, wind of a wild party, plans, time
on someone's hands.
Indoors it seemed so unbelievably red

against the open-plan, the forty
shades of grey; the flat lights
of our terminals. Fastened
at the window, it was seen
from every cubicle, and you'd realize
it had held your gaze for a full five minutes
or, absently, would catch yourself
just doodling a picture of it.

It has lived here for a week.
It has shrunk, now, like a soft fruit
and no one has the heart to remove it.
Once or twice we lift our heads and look
to where a finch or a blue tit,
hopelessly confused, attracted,
pits and blurs its wings against the glass
and fails and fails to taste it.

Bubble

(for Dan McAteer, 2)

My birth was easy as a breath.
He dreamt me up with an almost kiss.
I came to pass.
I came to float, drift,
exist for him as one clear thought
neatly caught in a soft glass case.

Amazed,
he stumbles now, gives chase
around and around
in shrieked delight,
both of us
just gifts of this new light

where I contain him,
and his eyes, wide, reflect me.
Each to each, we fascinate,
hypnotize and captivate:
his small hands reach for me
but cannot grasp a mystery

so colourful and pliable
yet utterly untouchable
on pain of death –
the moment of distress
as short-lived as happiness.
He will replace me.

Hayleigh and the Beanstalk

Home alone on the fourteenth floor with nothing
to do but stare at the view the social worker
so admires, you come kicking at my door.
They've shaved your hair, your spun-gold hair,
like a little prisoner of no war.

You take me back to the time before,
to the night your dad who had not been out
of the flat for four years, almost five,
stood up, clutched his chest, and died –
you tell me it was like *Casualty*, on the TV;

that you're looking out for that jelly-bean tree
I said would sprout when you cried when you dropped
your sweets through the bars of the balcony.
How I wish I could believe me
that unlike Jack you will climb down, out of the sky,

into real life.

The Trick

Jamie is up on the roof again. Jamie is up
on the raised edge, one mucky trainer raised
for his next balletic step,

skinny arms at east and west, a bound twig
cross of himself, little spindle weathervane
against a metal sky

where an errant gust, a warning shout
might spin him to the ground, spin him
down like a winged sycamore pod,

down to where a mother stands,
slack-jawed and motionless, to where
a mother stands and wills the whole world

motionless.

The Pines

All around,
the tapering pines
teeter, teeter,
jittery,
and with good cause
on a ground crossed
and counter-crossed
with the fallen,
that seem to sink,
are slowly lost
to a lush mess
of grasses, mosses.

Each is born
to bow and die
but one will tilt,
from time to time,
awkwardly
to another's arms
and, through the dark,
a met tension
seeks out
its release in sound.

Lovers
and insomniacs,
keepers
of the secret hours,
lift your heads
and listen, listen;
some will know
the low glissando
worked on the fretboard
of the night; some,
the call of one
speared soul
under a fearful,
startling moonlight.

The Dark

Invisible, but massive still,
the mountains
are components of it:
night creatures
audible in the grass,
the nerve and impulse of it;
day creatures
hushed in the warmth of nests
you suppose are its soft breath
and the bare trees
that were gesturing in the air
its veins,
if still there
of course. Birds
you've never seen,
scraps cut from the cloth of it,
are the thoughts of it
so every thing
surrenders now to the power of it,
gifts itself as a part of it,
but you.
You fight,
hold to your core of electric light,
active against it.

Gallery

She showed me the red earth
breaking under lightning, lightning
or else a great tear in the sky,
and I covered my eyes.
She played for me the small sounds
of white flame trembling,
the murmur of shadows
slanting from a roof, but I deafened
to her, and still wouldn't look.

When she took me
into the room of cloud
I closed the doors of my coat
around me, but she touched my arm
and she leaned to me, and put her mouth
to my mouth, lightly. There were
slate blue waves and nine ships
tilting where she left me, weighed
in the balance, wanting.

Tense

Like dry ice on a dance floor, the mist
pours over the river, ghost-
advances onto the land, over the walls
and darkened lawns, pressured
gently at the glass. Restless
in our separate beds, with only a mile
of mist between us, do we recall

or anticipate this; the first impulse,
chance opening, where one of us
will risk everything, leaned
and meets the other's lips, our mouths
fusing, hands unfastening clothes,
uncovering shoulders, breasts, burned
deeper and deeper in the kiss.

And was it you or I who will rise, later,
throw the windows wide, and let
the mist, persistent all the while,
fill the room where we lie
streamed in each other, breath in breath,
settled itself unbearably soft
on our nakedness in the moments after.

Blackbird

Love was discovered in air,
quick up-gusts like the brushstrokes
of God. We paired,

worked together in faith,
crafted out of the love
a nest, fibres of the love
enough, becoming wood,
compacted, tough.

We lined the nest – a thousand
blades of love turned
soft – and slept.

So we had love to give
when it came to the drum roll
of the dawn, could offer up
our blackbird love
in song.

Song for a Stone

(after Iain Crichton Smith)

You are at the bottom of my mind
like a stone dropped once by chance in a pool
to the black belied
by a surface ruled
by a total reflection of sky.

I do not have the know of your want or why,
I do not have the know of your way.
I have only the flow
of the come what may
in the light to the front of my liquid eye.

But you have put a sadness in the blue-
green waters of my mind
for as long as we both may live.

For your time is not of the colour of mine
and the name that is on you cannot be written
over these lips in love.

telephone?

Riddle

As much as you confide in me,
if you think that I'll be coming back
you're on the wrong track.
Our tryst will be intense but short.
I mean to travel, go abroad, so ask just this:
a single kiss, then one caress; no more, no less.

I wear my intentions clear as a coat, but a coat
of secrets to be kept – small betrayals, pleas
of the heart – all stuffed into its pocket's depth,
or stitched into its silk and hem.
My new love may just cut my throat,
or tear me apart, to discover them.

Words and Music

She moves about in the tiny flat
with the long strides of a goddess,
fixing this, or watering that,
mixing the books up, wearing my shirt.

She dials the little radio
through crashing waves of static,
through 'words, words, words!'
and finds a hidden symphony

then moves a chair to occupy
the single square of morning sun,
basks in the full length of herself,
ankles hooked on the window sill,

feet conducting sky. She asks me
if I love her. I wouldn't quite
go that far. It's just that
if she leaves me, I'm done for.

Lithium

In the photograph, you could be anybody
making the most of a bright bank holiday.
We could belong to any of those parked cars.

The children, netting for life at the edge
of the stillest, silver lake,
they could be ours.

What's the matter with us?

Only a tremor in the hand.
It rained, remember, after that, a rain
we couldn't see or feel but noticed,

dipping circles on the lake
as if it existed only in reflection,
as if inverse, beneath the surface tension.

The Seal

Where had you been? I can't remember.
Wherever it was, you were headed for home
on Charing Cross or Tottenham Court Road,
when the little silver handset tucked
in the breast pocket
of your denim jacket
took it upon itself to phone.

Hello, I said. *Hello . . . hello?*
and heard from underneath your clothes
a sound like breakers folding into foam
on shifting stones,
on a stretch of shingle,
a shore, perhaps, like this one here
where I am, at last, unreachable;

a beach where the only remarkable thing
is the dark, mottled body of a seal,
untouched as yet by any creature,
and over which
someone has draped
a plastic sheet or a bin liner
like a jacket over a sleeping lover.

I might have been a concerned doctor
sitting there on our living-room floor,
head inclined to a stethoscope, alert
to a hint of the
odd or irregular, listening
for what seemed like forever
but was only, in fact, the bones of an hour.

Present Perfect

I have laid down a river, lilac   *chinese painting*
in some lights,
to dream of the other side
with its mist-mysterious hills.
I have added a heron, hunched
on the shore in his old, raddled coat
from the Sixties.
I have gifted years of appointment diaries
to the fire, watched
as they disappeared,
week by smouldering week.

All is well. Activity
is the task of starlings stripping a rowan,
people, near
but not too near.
In a drawer, tickets
for a flight
on some, vague, future date.
And you, you are here
but out somewhere; not far,
due back for dinner . . .

+

Through the cabin window's haze
we watch the black shadow of our plane
free itself from the undercarriage,
separate, then fall away.

With it falls the sunlit runway,
grids of crops and reservoirs, then all
the scattered glitter of a city
falls, the tattered coastline of a country

plunges out of view.
And just when you might expect to see
the globe in brilliant clarity,
cloud fills the tiny screen

and we, who haven't taken off
at all, wait, seatbelts on,
for the world to turn and return to us
as it always does, sooner or later,

to fix itself to the craft again
at a point marked with the shadow of a plane,
pencilled now on a runway, growing
larger under Irish rain.